TOP TIPS:
HANDLING DIFFICULT
BEHAVIOUR

Graham Finch
with contributions from Simon Barker and Elizabeth Leese

Copyright © 2005
First published 2005
ISBN 1 84427 127 7

Scripture Union, 207–209 Queensway,
Bletchley, Milton Keynes, MK2 2EB,
England
Email: info@scriptureunion.org.uk
Website: www.scriptureunion.org.uk

Scripture Union Australia
Locked Bag 2, Central Coast Business
Centre, NSW 2252
Website: www.scriptureunion.org.au

Scripture Union USA
PO Box 987,Valley Forge, PA 19482
Website: www.scriptureunion.org

The right of Graham Finch to be
identified as author of this work has
been asserted by him in accordance
with the Copyright, Designs and
Patents Act 1988.

British Library Cataloguing-in-
Publication Data.
A catalogue record of this book is
available from the British Library.

Printed and bound in Dorchester,
England by Henry Ling.

Logo and cover design:
www.splash-design.co.uk

Internal design:
www.splash-design.co.uk

Internal illustrations:
Colin Smithson

Scripture Union is an
international Christian charity working
with churches in more than 130
countries, providing resources to bring
the good news about Jesus Christ to
children, young people and families
and to encourage them to develop
spiritually through the Bible and
prayer.

As well as our network of volunteers,
staff and associates who run holidays,
church-based events and school
Christian groups, we produce a wide
range of publications and support
those who use our resources through
training programmes.

INTRODUCTION

This book's starting point is the importance of valuing children for who they are, however challenging their behaviour. It suggests strategies that children's workers in church, other concerned adults, parents and carers can try when faced with difficult behaviour. It offers hope to all!

Part One: Causes and types of difficult behaviour
Part Two: Shaping behaviour
Part Three: Practical Top Tips

Most of my working life has been spent advising on how best to handle children's behaviour. I'm used to people saying, 'This is the problem; what do I do about it?' (I even remember my wife saying to me when our own children were young, 'You're supposed to be the expert! What do I do?') My first reaction is to panic, wondering what on earth I can say that might help because the reality is that there are no quick-fix answers. However, there are many ways of approaching behaviour problems that can make a huge difference. You'll find lots of encouraging stories here and plenty of practical advice to support you. If you're experiencing problems handling difficult behaviour, you're not alone! If you are a parent, then you already know that you have one of the most difficult jobs in the world, with little preparation, instruction or pay.

If you are a church worker, involved with your group for one or two hours each week, or are running a residential children's holiday, then you also have a very tough job. You will know that some children who behave well enough at school and at home can be difficult to settle into the structure of a Sunday group, holiday or club. One distracting child can make such a difference to the whole group. So what can we do?

CAUSES AND TYPES OF DIFFICULT BEHAVIOUR

Here is one frequent question I am asked: 'Is children's behaviour worse now than in the past?' My usual answer is that children's behaviour is simply less controlled now than in the past.

If you ask any group of adults if they ever stole anything as a child, you will usually find that the majority have. It is important to remember the mischief we got up to as children, because this helps us to be one step in front of the young people we are now working with. It reminds us that a) we weren't perfect and b) there's nothing new under the sun! One thing is very clear – you do not have to teach children to misbehave, they do it easily enough without instruction.

> **Think about...**
>
> Try to remember some of the mischief you got up to as a child. Most of us just forget and it takes time to remember. Ask friends to do the same. Their memories will stimulate your memory.

After all, we are all sinners! But without positive input, rules and adult guidance, mischief can make everyone's life a misery.

Some causes of challenging and disruptive behaviour

- **General learning difficulties**

Many children struggle in a learning situation, which may be how they perceive a Sunday group or children's club. Whatever the nature of their difficulty, they may associate your group too much with school and that makes them uncomfortable. Try to see it from their point of view. Of course, not all children with learning difficulties are negative towards school, especially if they have positive support. For more on this, read *Top Tips: Welcoming Special Children* – see inside front cover for details.

- **Specific learning difficulties with literacy or numeracy**

Some children (and adults) have a specific problem with patterns and symbols, finding it hard to remember the order and shape of letters and numbers. This means they find it hard to be organised. They may do something to divert attention, not wanting to show their insecure handwriting, reading and number skills in front of their peers. They do not enjoy worksheets or written word games.

- **Low self-image**

Many children have a very low opinion of themselves and this impacts on their behaviour. They want to be accepted but they do not know how to take the appropriate steps to build relationships. They may be uncooperative or attention-seeking. They may have lost all sense of where they belong in life and what gives them value. They may lack confidence and feel stressed, anxious and depressed. Emotional literacy, which is our ability to manage ourselves and our emotions and to understand other people's emotions, may be delayed. They may not understand forgiveness and trust because they have not experienced it. They may blame others/institutions/circumstances and may show no remorse. They may have personality traits that are not attractive.

They may be caught in a vicious circle. Their challenging behaviour brings negative relationships ➞ lack of rewards and compliments ➞ poor performance ➞ lowered self-image ➞ anxiety/insecurity ➞ challenging behaviour ➞

Just think about the power of the message that God loves and accepts them!

Think about...

A worthwhile book to read on this subject is Stephen Biddulph, *Raising boys*, Thorsons, 1997.

- **Developmental disorders**

Remember that these are lifetime disorders that can impair life at home, school and work and frustrate interpersonal relationships. A look at the websites that support the individual and the family will prove very informative.

The range of problem behaviours for those with Attention Deficit Hyperactivity Disorder is extensive. Impulsiveness, restlessness, inattentiveness, disorganisation and over-activity may be present. There is much debate and concern at the moment about labels such as ADHD and the use of medication. A number of parents I have met seem relieved that a diagnosis has been given and they have a reason for the behaviour of their children. An important factor that can so easily be overlooked, however, is that the behaviour still needs to be managed.

The difficulties of those with Autistic Spectrum Disorders are in the areas of language and communication, social relationships and limitations in imagination (with inflexibility of thought) and creative play. Young people with dyslexic and dyspraxic tendencies often struggle to cope with all the information around them and cannot 'multi-task'.

People with Auditory Processing Disorders fail to process part or all of an auditory message. They are not able to make sense of what they hear although they do not have a hearing loss.

- **Fragmented home situations and unsettled relationships with parents**

An increasing number of families are divided and lack stability. Many children carry around inside them an enormous amount of sadness and tension. Their lives may lack routine and security. How does a child find the words to articulate how they feel when a parent moves out of the family home? How does a child cope with spending time split between two homes, building relationships with a new stepfamily? Challenging behaviour is one option.

• Lack of boundaries in the home

As we have already said, parenting is a tough job and many parents struggle, especially if their own experience of being parented was poor or if life is just one long battle. Some children know too much about adult concerns and others are not prepared enough for the world. Some children receive a lot of negative stimulation from unsupervised video viewing and computer games. Children may not know how to behave in a small group and are only learning about this at school. They have not got the social skills to interact well. Good behaviour is taught as well as caught. We ought not to point a finger of accusation at parents but we will need to recognise the impact this can have and we can work towards creating boundaries of acceptable behaviour.

> **Think about...**
>
> Think of each of the children in your group. What might be the reason they misbehave?

• Physical demands

Life for everyone is pressurised and children of all ages experience this. The pressure to do well, to succeed, and to cope with all the demands placed upon them takes its toll. Poor quality diets and lack of exercise can also lead to tiredness, lethargy and irritating behaviour. Children without a regular routine may just not be in bed long enough to get adequate sleep. Some children may not sleep well because they are unhappy or a sibling disturbs them. Saturday night sleepovers often mean that children in a group on Sunday morning are switched off or disruptive.

- **Group dynamics**

This is an especially important consideration for children who are new to the Christian setting where you meet. If a child feels uncomfortable, they may behave badly. On the first day of a residential or holiday club, be especially aware of this and gently lay down guidelines for acceptable behaviour. For regular groups, a certain child in the group may annoy the others. They bring unresolved school and home disputes with them.

- **The organisation of your session**

You probably did not think of this at first! If we are not well prepared with appropriate activities, unacceptable behaviour may result. We may be the cause of a child's or group's behaviour.

Types of behaviour

James Dobson in *Dare to Discipline* (Kingsway 1972) puts behaviour into three categories.

- **Childish irresponsibility**

These are the silly things children do: spill drinks, dirty clean clothes, forget what they have been told, trip over nothing, break things or get into arguments over what appear to be very unimportant things. The reality is they do not do them on purpose, it 'just happens'.

It's important to remember that children do not do these silly things deliberately to annoy anyone. While they need to be dealt with, we must see them in the context of more serious aspects of behaviour. Being aware of this might ease some of the strain we can experience with children we work with.

> **In reality…**
>
> I have lost count of the number of occasions when people have recognised that most of the childish behaviour they were concerned with fell into this category. To discover the children were not doing it on purpose greatly improved relationships.

• Behaviour linked to development

Children develop at different speeds, and the skills they require for various tasks come bit by bit. Has the child physically, emotionally or mentally developed the skill we are requiring them to undertake? If there is a problem, check with their parent. They know their child better than anyone. A child may not be choosing to be difficult but just struggling to accomplish what has been asked of them.

• Challenge to authority

This is the more serious aspect of children's behaviour. Defiance and stubbornness come into this category. In this situation, the child is usually aware of what they are up to. We give an instruction, which we expect to be carried out. The child takes a stand against us and says, 'No'. Or it may be we have instructed them not to do something and they deliberately do precisely what we have told them not to do. The challenge is: 'What are you going to do about it?'

Many of us seem to back away from this challenge only to find that the child challenges more and more frequently. When the child has challenged a parent and got away with it they will then challenge others in authority, including teachers, any adult and, of course, church workers. It is important to see that this is not to be taken personally and is not aimed at just the children's worker.

This challenge needs to be met and won by both parents and workers or the child's behaviour will make life miserable for everyone. The truth is that children want and need enforced boundaries. Without this structure to life they feel insecure, unhappy and afraid of their own power. We can and must take control and later on we will look at exactly how to do this. Children will still continue to test us out but that's OK. It is part of a need to explore and test what is acceptable.

As we said before, we do not have to teach children to be 'naughty' – they can do that without any help. However, we do purposefully have to teach them to be good, to do what is right. Young children in particular will often ask the simple question: 'Have I been good today?' They will know what is 'naughty' because so often we make an issue of it but they are not always clear what being 'good' is. Good behaviour is not just exceptional behaviour such as tidying a bedroom without prompting and tackling homework without being sat on. For me, good behaviour is behaviour that is not naughty.

I have often heard people remark, 'He's only attention seeking, ignore him.' If a child is seeking attention it is because he needs attention. (This is not ADHD.) Children may choose an inappropriate way to gain it but they still need attention. If you face this difficulty, deliberately look for a way to give attention to the child for something positive, no matter how small, before they swing into inappropriate behaviour. It really is worth the effort and the pay-off is huge, not only for the worker but also for the child.

Children love and need adult attention. There are two ways of gaining that. Either we can ignore children when they are being good, partly because we feel that is the way they should behave anyway. Then it does not take long for them to recognise that

they get far more attention when they are naughty. Or we put our energy into positively acknowledging children when they are being good. Then they know more clearly what we mean by 'good' behaviour and we discover how effective praise is for changing behaviour.

> **In reality...**
>
> Lisa always wanted to be the one chosen to do anything in the holiday club and to be close to the leader. She longed for attention. The others in her group got fed up with her. One day the leader announced that Lisa was to be her special helper. She gave her a couple of boring tasks that she had prepared beforehand. Lisa had to stay close to the leader to do these. It was not long before she got bored and asked to join the others. She had felt special for a short time, the other children had not wanted to do these tasks and then she chose to move out of the limelight.

Children who are taken notice of when they are being good soon begin to understand that this behaviour is worth repeating.

Labelling

'The naughty child'

In a school, residential holiday, church group or club, a naughty child can get labelled as 'difficult' or 'naughty'. Once the label is made, it is difficult to remove. A bad start easily becomes a bad name. Adults may find it hard to accept a different label on a child. What is more, children can live up to their label whether it is 'good', 'weak', 'stupid' or 'helpful'. If they have lived with that label for a long time, they get so used to it that they find it very difficult when someone relates to them in a different way. That's why a child who is naughty will immediately go and do something naughty when someone praises them, in order to maintain the image they are used to. Changing this takes time, patience and persistence. It is easy to give up too soon.

I met a large family where one of the boys was labelled 'naughty' and one of the girls was the 'good' child. I spent some time with them

and was surprised when the 'good girl' stated, 'I always have to be good. That's what everyone expects. I'd love to be naughty sometimes.' The 'naughty' boy said, 'Everyone expects me to be naughty, so I am. I would like to be good sometimes but they won't let me.'

SHAPING BEHAVIOUR

2

I know all this emphasis on discipline may seem a bit heavy for working with children in a church context but Hebrews 12:6 reminds us of the importance of these things and includes this statement: 'The Lord disciplines those he loves, and he punishes everyone he accepts as a son.' (NIV) We should not be afraid to discipline children. It is actually an important way of expressing our love for them. Discipline ought to be more about training and modelling than about punishment.

Children who are appropriately and lovingly disciplined are more secure, more accepted in society and more integrated. They are more likely to have a sense of well-being and they usually find success.

> **Think about...**
>
> 'A child left to himself disgraces his mother' (Proverbs 29:15) (NIV). You only have to listen to the way an undisciplined child talks to his/her mother to know this is true. Take time to listen to this type of interaction next time you go shopping.

For the past 40 years I have worked with parents and children in a variety of settings. I am convinced that undisciplined children are unhappy children and cause everyone they come into contact with to be affected by their unhappiness.

We believe that all children are made in the image of God. They matter to him, so much so that he was prepared to send his son to die for each and every one of them! Since children matter that much to him, we too ought to see a child (and indeed everyone) as someone valued by God. This means that we will want to show children how much we value them.

A God-focused attitude to every child will mean that we are actively looking for the positive things that each child has said or done. We will ensure that we do not run games, quizzes or activities that put a child down. We will truthfully praise a child for who she is. It is important that what we say is true, for children are quick to recognise insincerity. This mindset of praising and valuing is something every children's worker needs to develop. Coincidentally, it is also a useful tool for encouraging good behaviour.

When we were in residential care work, I was the 'house father' and my wife, Jeanne, was the nurse in the sickbay. Some of the senior boys I had to look after were quite a handful. I said to Jeanne, 'Let me know if you have any trouble with them.' Her reply caught me by surprise. 'I don't have problems with them, they are lovely.' 'Lovely' is not how I would have described them! I was puzzled until I was down in the sickbay one evening when many of my 'difficult' youngsters arrived to see the nurse. As soon as they showed their face around the door Jeanne had a positive comment to make about them. I watched them melt before my eyes.

Some people have the strange idea that praising someone will make them big-headed. But, of course, we all need praise. We all need to be told when we have done well. I was encouraged when I read the story of Jesus in Luke 3:22: 'A voice came from heaven: "You are my Son, whom I love; with you I am well pleased."' (NIV) I wonder how Jesus felt after that. I imagine that after that affirmation, he felt secure as he entered the wilderness to undergo a time of testing.

Jesus wanted the children to know him, to know he was there for them. Jesus discouraged the barriers and excuses that the disciples suggested to keep the children away.

The challenge is for us to keep asking ourselves the question: what would Jesus do?

Getting started

• Working within the church community

If you are working within a church context, you are part of a wider community. It is important for your Christian fellowship to have clear structures within which you work. There should be a clear Child Protection Policy for everyone involved with children and, within this, clear guidelines on dealing with challenging behaviour. If these are not in place, you should talk to your church leadership about establishing them.

Similarly, it is clearly not appropriate under any circumstances for children in a church-organised activity to be smacked by workers. The Child Protection Policy in your church should give clear guidelines on any form of physical contact with children. Neither is it good practice for leaders to become aggressive, to express anger or to shout at children.

Lord Laming, in his report on the Victoria Climbie inquiry, pointed out that not only did the Police, Social Services, Housing Department, Hospitals and NSPCC fail to help and protect Victoria, but she had also been taken to several churches. We need to bear in mind that the church is the largest voluntary organisation working with children and therefore, out of our love for children we must ensure their protection.

In reality...

This is what a Christian couple who adopted four brothers and sisters with ADHD said:
'We want to thank the people in our church for...

- supporting us through the school exclusions and AWOLs
- sitting in our pew or asking the children to sit with them
- welcoming our disturbed children and giving them responsibilities
- seeing the child and not the distracting behaviour
- letting us talk about our exhaustion and worries.'

It can be very difficult to see positive things in children and young people whose behaviour is extremely difficult, and especially if you feel negative about the children themselves. It needs both prayer and a determination that the situation can be different. This is one of the reasons why being part of a team together is so important. We need to support each other in thinking positively about each child in our care. One Sunday group leader feeling unappreciated and working on her own, became negative and unable to appreciate and enjoy the children. Once she felt appreciated and began to work more closely with others, her attitude changed completely!

- **Working with the parent(s)**
We must never lose sight of the fact that usually, parents are the prime carers of their children. What framework is there in your church to consult with parents? Parents often need support and encouragement which could well come from those of us who work with

their children. It is important to find out what parents' expectations are in dealing with the behaviour of their child because we do not want to undermine the situation at home.

One of the major problems I have encountered when working with parents is where mum and dad are not in agreement on what behaviour is acceptable and what is not. Rules within the home and how to punish children may vary between parents. This will affect a child's expectation of discipline in your group.

In reality…

Leaders on a residential holiday want to keep in contact with the children. Great care needs to be taken not to undermine the discipline within the child's home, even if a child may grumble about parents. Of course, disclosure of abuse is a different matter altogether and has to be acted upon seriously.

- **Working with other children's workers**

All that is written here needs to be applied in a team context. Establishing rules and caring for your group is a team activity. It is good practice for no one adult to be alone with a group. You need to be in a team, working consistently together! Children soon spot the tensions and differences and will play adults in the group off against each other. It is a great game and one in which they are very skilled. Having an established framework for handling behaviour across all the groups adds to the security of adults and children.

3

PRACTICAL TOP TIPS

When thinking of ways to help a few children, we are challenged to think about the way we deal with the group. This may well lead to the whole group benefiting from a change in our approach.

Rule setting and rule keeping

What makes a good rule?
- It has to be clear
- It has to relevant
- It has to be achievable
- It has to be clearly communicated
- It has to be fair
- It has to be understood
- It can apply to the whole group or individuals
- It has to be positive (preferably)
- It has to be… add on other words that you think are appropriate

Think about...

Ask your team members what rules you think you have in your club or group. Write them down on a flip chart. You may be surprised what they come up with. Then ask your children to think up a good set of rules for the group. Again you may be surprised what they suggest.

Come to an agreement about the most suitable top ten rules and write them up for all to see. Each time you meet, this will act as a reminder. Children usually do not mind this. They are used to having lots to remember and rules differ from home to school to church. Some problems simply occur when they forget which rules apply where!

Consequences

Having established clear rules for your group, the next step is to decide what happens if the rule is broken. It is no good having rules if nothing happens when they are broken.

How many times have you witnessed the scene in your local shopping centre of a child touching something? The parent says, 'Don't touch that! Will you leave that alone? Behave!' The parent then turns to a friend and says, 'He never does anything I say.'

A major mistake, made by a parent or children's worker when there are no set, clear consequences, is to keep telling, nagging and warning until finally the adult gets really cross and hands out a 'punishment'. Spur of the moment punishments are usually a bit over the top, are not thought through and often are not relevant to training a child in the way he should go. It is especially important when working with a group of children in a church context that we do not mete out punishments that are not appropriate for the situation and damage the relationships being built in the group. Carrying punishments over from one week to the next is also damaging. Above all, children's workers must never lose out on an opportunity to be positive, guiding a child to an alternative option rather than imposing a punishment.

> **In reality...**
>
> I once asked foster carers what rules they had at home. They replied, 'Not many.' I then asked the children what they thought the rules were. They came up with a very long list, much to the amazement and embarrassment of the foster carers, who could only say, 'Yes, that's right. Yes, that's right.'

The other mistake is to make threats and not carry them out. You've probably heard an adult say, 'Stop it, or I'll ...' How serious was the adult? Often the child clearly knows when there is no serious intention of action being followed through.

Your options for sanctions include:

- to provide an alternative diversionary activity
- to set a child to work with a different group of children
- to take time out to cool down or provide a quiet area
- to provide some individual attention (without giving the impression that this is a reward for bad behaviour)
- to set up a system of 'yellow' cards as a warning of the consequences
- to use the ultimate sanction of exclusion

Once you have settled on the consequences of breaking a rule, enforce that consequence every time the rule gets broken. Be patient. Do not increase or change the consequence. Unacceptable behaviour is rarely stopped in one go. The best approach is to aim to reduce it over a period of time until the rule becomes internalised.

It may be that the bad behaviour will actually increase a little in the early stages as the child really tests the boundaries. Don't panic! Keep going and be determined you can succeed. After a while, you will find they have internalised the rule. It has become part of them.

You may want to involve the children in a group discussion about the consequences of broken rules. Be prepared for outrageous responses with some really tough 'punishments' which you will want to discuss and moderate!

Be aware that excluding a child has an impact on more than just the child. It may not help the parent (who may be struggling anyway) to have their child returned to them in a service or in disgrace during club-time. Is there somewhere else or with someone else that a child can go, which is safe but is perceived as a firm deterrent? Talk about this with your colleagues.

Think about...

Ask yourself if you really need all the rules you have drawn up? Do they have any real meaning? Check them out again. Then discuss what sanctions and punishments you have at your disposal.

A reminder

Do not be afraid to impose guidelines. It is in the child's own interest, the group's interest and your own too. As part of demonstrating love to the children in our care, we need to provide structure and equip them for all the challenges of life ahead – like jobs and relationships. We want them to feel happy and confident in themselves as they grow.

Expressing positive and truthful things to children about themselves can make all the difference as we have already seen.

Even the best observed rules do not necessarily bring about the behaviour we want, but they can limit the level of bad behaviour.

The motivation to change sometimes has to be encouraged by rewarding positive behaviour. The best way to reward is by simply expecting good behaviour and showing you enjoy it. A group reward such as an extra ten minutes of football or a song everyone enjoys is more affirming than rewarding the good child, which has the negative effect of demotivating the child who struggles to behave!

Top tips to encourage appropriate behaviour

Good preparation. Be well prepared for your session. Children should have the best, not the leftovers of our time and attention.

This may sound obvious but spend time **praying** over the session and for each child who attends by name. Spend time in the room you are using and pray in the room for God's blessing.

I ran a Family Centre for 15 years in a deprived area of Coventry. During that time I regularly walked round the building praying that God would bless everyone who entered, that they might know God and his peace and blessing in their lives. It was wonderful how often visitors commented, 'It's so peaceful when you walk in, it leaves you feeling relaxed.' Prayer makes a profound difference in the lives of the children we work with.

Be first in the room and make sure everything is in place before the children arrive so that you are ready to greet the children individually. Don't have your back to them as they enter. Face them, look at them, greet them, smile at them and welcome them. Make sure you have an achievable introductory activity for them.

Make sure there is a **place for quiet** chats. Some children will arrive bursting with energy, others will be restless, tired or sad. Some will want to be quiet, others to race around. Cater for all these moods. Music is an effective way to provide a calm environment. You have to choose how and when to use it, but quiet background music can quieten everyone down.

Help the children feel they are **accepted** unconditionally. Speak positively to them whenever possible: 'Your hair is always beautiful', 'You're great at telling jokes' and 'I like the way you do that.' Negative comments damage the spirit of a child and lead to many problems later on.

Give clear specific instructions.

Avoid making comparisons with others in the group and don't have favourites. It is easy to fall into this trap. One child is always attentive, helpful, knowledgeable and responsive. If we focus too much on this child we are almost saying to the others, 'Why can't you be like this?' The rest will instinctively react.

In reality...

A colleague visited a home where the relationship between mother and son had completely broken down. It seemed impossible to change and it looked as though the child might have to be taken into care. My colleague asked the boy what he liked about his mother. His immediate reply was, 'She makes great lemon meringue pies.' This was the chink in the door and from that point onward they began to explore the positives about each other. This changed the whole atmosphere and ultimately prevented the boy being taken into care.

Use the children's **names** often.

Alert them if there will be **changes** to the routine.

Choose your battles carefully. One expression of irritating behaviour may not be the one to home in on.

Get to know each child well. They are very interesting, unique individuals. Remember what you all talked about last week and ask further questions. The formation of a good relationship with the children in your care can make an incredible difference to behaviour within the session.

Plan for the full length of the session and have reserve activities. The way you structure your activities, the materials you use and the enthusiasm you show, will considerably reduce any behaviour difficulties. Don't give the children the chance to get bored and therefore behave badly. Have plenty of things to do with lots of fun, interaction and laughter.

Remember that many may have poor concentration.

Offer choices within an acceptable range.

Use a **voice** in between a shout and a whisper.

Occasionally, do something **totally different**, for example, rearrange all the furniture or set everything a different way round. (Make sure your group are settled and secure with you before trying this.) Wear the occasional unusual outfit or bring in a visitor. If possible, get outside the confines of your normal room.

A word of warning: **Avoid punishing the whole group** for the behaviour of a few. It does happen. I've seen it. But it can be very destructive and is just not an appropriate or fair way of handling a group of children.

Expressing positive and truthful things to children about themselves can make all the difference as we have already seen.

You could arrange a handling **children's behaviour course** for parents of children in your group. A number

Think about...

Look at a list of all the children in your club or group. Identify at least one positive thing you could say to each child. How and when will you be able to do this? Review your last time together with the children. How often did you point out the negative things a child did which may have overshadowed five positive ones!? Talk with your colleagues about this to get their feedback. It is a very valuable exercise to do together.

of churches use one of these courses as a means of service and outreach to the community. There are many good ones available.

I have been working on a project over the past few years to make a free course on handling children's behaviour available to all parents in the City of Coventry. For more details visit www.FutureChildcareTraining.com

Think about...

If you are working with older children and teenagers, look at *Responding to Challenging Behaviour* Grove Books, Youth Series No 1 (2005) for plenty of additional advice and information.

Form a relationship with parents. You are working to support them and are on their side. Never lose sight of that. Get to know them and find out about their children. It may well be that they are struggling with their child's behaviour too. It also helps when the child knows you talk to their parents.

Top tips on dealing with specific problem behaviour

It is all too easy to generalise so do a bit of specific analysis and ask yourself:

- Who is this behaviour a problem for?
- What exactly is the problem?
- Is there a pattern? When does the problem behaviour occur? A certain time?
- Where does it occur? A certain place/activity?
- What is the trigger? Why might it occur?
- How might it be resolved?

Ask the parent if their child is like this with everyone and if there is one place they go where they are different. Explore their answer further. Talk to anyone in your congregation who may have some relevant experience. Get someone to **observe** and take notes in some detail of the child's behaviour in your session (with the parent's permission). This would be even better if you could do this over a number of sessions. Study your results, for you may well be surprised at what you find and this could lead to a revised approach to the child or group.

Prevent escalation and avoid threats. Don't allow yourself to be drawn into bargaining with a child who is determined to cause trouble. The situation will quickly spiral downwards! Threats will be made that cannot be kept.

Minimise aggression. Never resort to violence and try to deflect the strong emotion of a child who is getting worked up by providing diversions.

In reality...

When working at Child Guidance some years ago, there were families who would attend the centre with their child who had been diagnosed as hyperactive. Within a few minutes the waiting area would be wrecked. However, I made an interesting discovery when I asked the question, 'Is your child like this with everyone or is there one place they go where they are different?' In the majority of cases the answer was, 'Yes, he's different when he is with so-and-so.' That was a clue for us to explore: how did that person handle the child?

Use **gentle humour**, never sarcasm or put-downs.

Correct confusions. Much bad behaviour is a result of children not understanding, not hearing properly or not reading the communication clues they have been given. Ask the child to explain what they think has gone wrong or has led them to feel aggrieved.

Acknowledge improvements. As ever, be always looking out for the child who has made an effort and let them know how pleased you are.

Explain from your point of view why something is problem behaviour. 'I was sad and disappointed when you put your fist up to Jim. We were all getting on well and it was a friendly atmosphere. Jim is cross now.' Help the troublemaker to see a cause-effect link.

Do not ignore the withdrawn child who does not cause any trouble but who may have serious problems that are overlooked.

Top tips for yourself as a children's worker

Have **reasonable expectations** of yourself and the group and be prepared to be surprised.

Form a **prayer support** group. Ask one of your church prayer groups to commit to praying for your group or club. Give them regular updates and prayer requests. They will pray for the group and you too!

Work alongside other leaders and alongside the children too. You are not called to be a confronter!

Pray very specifically for a difficult child. If the parent is a Christian, encourage them to pray over the child while they are asleep every night for a period and watch the difference.

It is very moving, challenging and humbling to hear a child describe the struggles she faces. **Expect to learn** things yourself as you handle the difficult behaviour of the children.

Remember – **we all make mistakes** and mess up on occasion. Forgive yourself, take courage and try again.

Ask for help. If you are stuck, struggling with a situation or child, be honest, swallow your pride and ask for help. There will be other experienced people who can look objectively at the situation with you and you will learn something for the future.

Specific points relating to residential holidays

The principles in this book have been written primarily with church groups and clubs in mind. But the advice and principles largely apply to residential holidays too. Here are some specific points for those leading such activities.

1. Get as much information as possible in advance. On the booking form, ask about behavioural or social problems.

2. Prevention is better than cure. Ensure that clear expectations are set in pre-holiday material and reinforced at the outset of the event.

3. Make sure there is always a structure to the programme with sufficient supervision. Unsupervised 'free time' is a recipe for disaster. (The 30 minutes' gap after the evening meal, when the leaders are tired or washing up, is a common time for incidents to happen.)

4. Involve parents where necessary. Some children can 'try it on' when they are away from home but if they know you are serious about contacting parents, it may act as a major deterrent to others, as well as resolve the issue with the child who is misbehaving.

5. Remember that your duty of care to the group outweighs your duty of care to the individual. So if a child is particularly disruptive, to the extent that their behaviour is incompatible with the general safety and enjoyment of others (including the adult team), they should be sent home. This is not a failure. It is simply a recognition that some young people require more trained supervision than is available. Far better they leave with the potential of returning next time than letting them

stay, out of a misguided sense of altruism. Make sure you have contact details for parents and can get the child home if the carer can't or won't collect their child.

Final words

For some reason this generation has almost become afraid to discipline children but this only leads to many children being at best insecure, and at worst damaged, and prevented from reaching their full potential.

All good children's work affirms and values children for who they are, long before comment is passed on what they have done. This is because God values us in that way.

In order for children to feel secure, they need clear boundaries and rules. The consequences for broken rules need to be clear and implemented when necessary. It is important for us to be consistent and fair. If the children were involved in drawing up the rules and consequences, they would be more likely to own them. These are good foundations on which all other approaches are built.

Boundaries (rules with consequences) will reduce the behaviour you don't want but will not give you the behaviour you do want. Good behaviour has to be modelled and taught and encouraged with praise and affirmation.

Remember there are usually no quick-fixes. Very rarely is unacceptable behaviour changed instantly. Behaviour problems are usually habits that have been formed over time and like all habits, such as biting nails, they take time to break. The most effective way of changing unacceptable behaviour is to aim to reduce it over a period of time.

Get to know the children and their parents very well, pray for them regularly, speak to them and bring good things into their lives. You are in partnership with the parents. And you are part of a team within your church or group so the responsibility for the nurture and discipline of the children is a shared one!

God disciplines us because he loves us, so we must be the channel of God's love and our own love too as we manage the behaviour of the children in our care.